I AM ENOUGH

14-DAYS OF SELF-WORTH, STRENGTH, & ENCOURAGEMENT

Chantelle L. Bittings, LCPC, NCC

Copyright © 2018 Chantelle L. Bittings

Book Package and Publication: Dr. Lawanne' S. Grant
Leadership DevelopME, LLC: www.leadershipdevelopme.com

All rights reserved. No part of this book may be used or reproduced by any means, graphic, electronic, or mechanical, including photocopying, recording, taping or by any information storage retrieval system without the written permission of the publisher except in the case of brief quotations embodied in critical articles and reviews.

Books may be ordered through booksellers or by contacting:

Chantelle L. Bittings
Website: www.cbittingstherapy.com

Because of the dynamic nature of the Internet, any web addresses or links contained in this book may have changed since publication and may no longer be valid. The views expressed in this work are solely those of the author and do not necessarily reflect the views of the publisher, and the publisher hereby disclaims any responsibility for them.

Any people depicted in stock imagery provided by Thinkstock are models, and such images are being used for illustrative purposes only.
Certain stock imagery © Thinkstock.

ISBN: 978-0-359-15988-8
Library of Congress Control Number: 2018961787

Printed in the United States of America

Scripture taken from The Holy Bible, KJV 1769 edition, public domain. Scriptures taken from ESV (English Standard Version) is adapted from the Revised Standard Version of the Bible, copyright Division of Christian Education of the National Council of the Churches of Christ in the U.S.A. Scripture quotations marked MSG are taken from *THE MESSAGE*, copyright © 1993, 1994, 1995, 1996, 2000, 2001, 2002 by Eugene H. Peterson. Used by permission of NavPress. All rights reserved. Represented by Tyndale House Publishers, Inc. Scriptures marked AMP are taken from the AMPLIFIED BIBLE (AMP): Scripture taken from the AMPLIFIED® BIBLE, Copyright © 1954, 1958, 1962, 1964, 1965, 1987 by the Lockman Foundation Used by Permission. (www.Lockman.org). Scriptures marked NKJV are taken from the NEW KING JAMES VERSION (NKJV): Scripture taken from the NEW KING JAMES VERSION®. Copyright© 1982 by Thomas Nelson, Inc. Used by permission. All rights reserved.

TABLE OF CONTENTS

Dedication i

Foreword iv

Introduction 1

Day 1: **I AM** supposed to be here 5

Day 2: **I AM** secure 11

Day 3: **I AM** significant 17

Day 4: **I AM** loved 29

Day 5: **I AM** chosen 35

Day 6: **I AM** God's beautiful creation 41

Day 7: **I AM** strong 47

Day 8: **I AM** capable 53

Day 9: **I AM** bold 59

Day 10: **I AM** living with purpose 65

Day 11: **I AM** forgiven 71

Day 12: **I AM** at peace 77

Day 13: **I AM** whole..83

Day 14: **I AM** me and **I AM** enough......................................87

Conclusion 93

Author's Bio 95

DEDICATION

Writing this dedication is like speaking at a testimony service. So first, I give honor to God who is the head of my life. It's cliché but so true. God is truly the reason I am who I am and why I do what I do. I am thankful for His hand in my life.

This book is dedicated to the memory of my grandfather, Dr. John Albert Jones, Jr. He was an ordinary man, greatly used by God. He meant so much to so many. To me, he was Granddaddy. He had a way of making us all feel we were his favorites. I think he knew that I needed a little more love, a little more nurturing, and a little more reassurance. I thank him for always making me feel special and that I was enough, even as a child. I dedicate this book to his love, life, and legacy.

To my mommy, your confidence in me has always pushed me to greatness. Your strength, determination, and pure grit have taught me some of life's most important lessons. You are one of the most hardworking women that I know. Thank you for your love and friendship. God truly smiled on me when He gave me to you. Thank you, Daddy, for your tough love. You taught me to never settle and to always plan. Your love for all of us is unmeasurable.

To my sisters and brothers, Chenoa and Abbiw, Dishon and Kim, Gregory and Aisha, Brandis and Justin, and Brian and Ashleigh, your support means the world to me. I love you all. Chenoa, my baby sister and bestie, thanks for the daily phone calls, the moments that you let me vent and the laughs we share. I also want to thank my sons, Thomas Jr. and Gaston. Thank you for being brilliant children who make being a mom, the best job in the world.

A special thank you to anyone who has ever sat on my couch, thank you for trusting me with your trials, tragedies, and triumphs. I am better because of you. Thank you to my pastor, Elder Osmond Jones and my Rehoboth Ministries Church of God in Christ family. To my running buddies, Grandma and Tee Tee Eva, I love you. Thanks to my MDT Sisters and my Harmony Sisters; you keep me grounded. My secret weapon, my photographer, PR rep, and sister, Cydni

Polk, you rock! Dr. Lawanne' Grant, your gentle nudges, and words of wisdom pushed me over the finish line. This is just the beginning!

To my dear husband, my life partner, and purpose pusher. Thank you will never suffice. I'm grateful for every day that you pick up our sons and allow me to continue to do the work that I love. I thank you for all the sacrifices that you have made for me to have a private practice. I thank you for all of the times you've said, "Go write baby; get it done." Your support, encouragement, and selfless love made me press on when I really wanted to just quit. Thank you for praying for me and constantly speaking God's Word over me. I say it all the time and it bears repeating, Thomas you are everything I wanted and everything I never knew I needed. I love you immensely.

FOREWORD

I get the opportunity to see you serve as a source of wisdom, strength, support, encouragement, and love — that's just what you do for me! In addition, you are a great mother to our two sons (as well as other "surrogate kids"), a great sister (by blood and through friendship), a mentor to many (both professionally and through life experiences) and a lover of God. How befitting it is to see you write this book to encourage others that they are enough, when you know first-hand how to complete people.

Even more than your extensive professional training and years of experience helping others, the anointing that God has placed in your life has equipped you to do great things. I'm excited to see your next chapter as you share this gift with God's people. Just as the other things you've set your hands to do, I'm sure He will make this come forth as pure GOLD!

I love you immensely and wish you great success in this endeavor. I'm grateful that you allow me to ride along on this fantastic voyage that God has set you on. Godspeed as you sail on to success in Him.

Yours in Christ and Love,
Thomas

INTRODUCTION

I have been a therapist in private practice for over ten years. During this time, I've noticed a recurring theme while working specifically with women who are learning to live their best lives. It seems that a great majority of women have yet to fully understand their self- worth.

Self-worth is much more than how you feel about yourself when you look in the mirror. It comes from a much deeper place. Self-worth is about knowing your authentic self. Self-worth is being comfortable with your gifts, talents, strengths, flaws, insecurities, and weaknesses. Self-worth is being able to say that despite all the struggles and deficiencies, I AM ENOUGH.

As women, we often question, compare, and doubt ourselves. We spend our days looking at social media outlets where people are faking on Facebook, imitating on Instagram, pining away on Pinterest, and tweeting on Twitter. It may seem almost impossible to form your own sense of self with these images constantly bombarding your mental landscapes. Your internal dialogue can sometimes be even more damaging than these outside influences. At times, it can convince you that you are not good enough, not smart enough, not qualified enough, too scarred, too damaged, and unworthy.

This internal dialogue is full of falsehoods that have been collected through your interactions with family, friends, and foes throughout your lifetime. Hence, you must overcome the lies that you tell yourself if you are ever going to say, I AM ENOUGH.

The absolutely best news of all is that God already knew the issues we would face. He has it all under control. Psalms 139: 13 (NKJV) says, "For You formed my inward parts; You covered me in my mother's womb." I take great comfort in knowing that before I allowed a single doubt or insecurity to take residence in my mind, God was already there.

As a Licensed Clinical Professional Counselor, a daughter of the King, and a woman who has struggled with self-worth, it is my hope that as you embark on these 14 days of study, you will be encouraged, and strengthened to declare loudly, I AM ENOUGH!

I AM ENOUGH

Day 1

I AM Supposed to Be Here

Who I AM

How did I get here? Have you ever sat in a room filled with important and revered people and wondered, how in the world you got a seat at the table? A feeling of dread creeps over you. You have a disconcerting feeling they will soon find out you should not have been invited. What if they find out you are not as great as they think? Sweat surfaces on your skin as you review your achievements and qualifications. You discount your education and positions you have held. You simply don't believe you are good enough. This is called the Imposter Syndrome.

If you are truly honest with yourself, at some point in life, you have been afraid that people will think you are a fraud. You may worry that you have gotten this far by luck or happenstance. You doubt your education, your experience, and your competency. So, you cower and shrink within yourself and really begin to question if you are supposed to be here.

At times, we all fall victim to what clinicians refer to as "Stinking Thinking." Stinking Thinking is when negative thoughts cycle and recycle through your mind. You have a hard time finding the silver lining in the clouds, and your glass is never half full. In fact, your glass has a long crack on the side. There is no light at the end of the tunnel and the sun will not come out tomorrow or the day after. Stinking Thinking traps you in a vicious cycle of hopelessness. The good news, my friend, is that none of this is true. Your purpose and the plan for your life have been predestined even before you were born.

Who Does God Say I AM?
"For I know the thoughts that I think toward you, saith the LORD, thoughts of peace, and not of evil, to give you an expected end" (Jeremiah 29:11, KJV).

God knew that you would be in this place before you arrived. Rest easy. Get comfortable. Get ready to SOAR!

Practical Application to Become Who I AM
Here are a few tips:
1. Celebrate your accomplishments. You have worked hard to get to this place in life.
2. Don't discount your achievements.
3. Accept the compliments; say thank you without any qualifiers.

Note to Who I AM
You are exactly where you should be. You have been uniquely and divinely qualified for this time and space. Walk in the favor God has allowed. Know that this is just the beginning.

"But as it written, Eye hath not seen, nor ear heard, neither have entered into the heart of man, the things which God hath prepared for them that love him" (I Corinthians 2:9, KJV).

This is the beginning of your journey. God has great things in store for you.

Thrive in who you've been called to be without apology.

LET'S WORK!

Make today your day of **Pure Positivity**. Don't allow any negative thoughts to occupy any space in your mind. Don't let any negative words come out of your mouth. That's right — no complaining, no arguing, no second-guessing yourself. Today, you will speak good things about you. By the end of the day, list 5 things you have done well.

1.

2.

3.

4.

5.

I AM ENOUGH

Day 2

I AM Secure

Who I AM

The great I AM reminded me that in Him, I am enough. I am secure. With His words of assurance, I finally figured out I am exactly who I should be.

My teenage years were messy. I exerted lots of energy trying to wear the "in clothes," listen to the "in music," and be with the "in crowd." I wasted so much time trying to fit in that I never considered maybe — I was meant to stand out. I often wonder how my life would have been different if I had just been comfortable in my own skin. I was never secure in being the me God created me to be.

Honestly, as a teen, I had no idea who I was. I didn't spend enough time with me to know my likes, dislikes, hopes, and dreams. I often put on a confident front when, in fact, I was shaking in my boots and hoping to be accepted. I wasn't sure of anything, and I especially wasn't sure of me.

Thankfully, since then, I've grown up a bit and realized that we were all just as unsure during our teen years. We were learning, growing, hopefully maturing, and figuring out this thing called life. I'm so grateful for the grace of God that covered and kept me through all my foolishness.

I find such great comfort in Psalm 138:8. God thinks so much about this little ol' gal (in my great- Grandma's voice) that He keeps me close to Him. There are so many times when I know I don't deserve His care; yet, He is always there. I am secure in Him.

So, my friend, I am secure not because of my high self-esteem that I have built. Instead, I am secure because I make every effort to stay close to the one who holds me close. He is my refuge and my hiding place.

Who Does God Say I AM?

Even still, in my moments of insecurity, God reminds me that in Him, I have all that I need. I am exactly who He intended me to be. Despite all the slips, falls, and mistakes that I was sure I could never recover from, He still had PURPOSE in it all. God has consistently reminded me that nothing can separate me from His love.

For I am persuaded, that neither death, nor life, nor angels, nor principalities, nor powers, nor things present, nor things to come. Nor height, nor depth, nor any other creature, shall be able to separate us from the love of God, which is in Christ Jesus our Lord (Romans 8:38-39, KJV).

Practical Application to Become Who I AM

Insecurity keeps you cemented in fear. It robs you of your power and your peace. When you feel insecure, it's easy to remain trapped in the "what ifs." What if I'm not smart enough, pretty enough or loved enough?

Insecurities can damage your relationships. When you are preoccupied with your insecurities — uncertain, anxious, lacking confidence in yourself — you can't see the needs of others. You find it very difficult to embrace the love they are extending to you.

My challenge to you is to make the following verbal declarations:
1. "No fear lives here."
2. "I am secure in God and His plan for my life."
3. "I will embrace genuine love extended by others and confidently give love that nurtures healthy and secure relationships."

Pause, take a step back; don't allow insecurity to be the reason you miss the love you are searching for and deserve to have.

Note to Who I AM
When you fully embrace this place of security, get ready to glow and grow. Your confidence and sparkle will propel you to heights unknown! Grow up and Glow up!

Thrive in who you've been called to *be* without *apology*.

LET'S WORK!

The best way to truly feel secure in where you are today is to really appreciate where you have been. Take a moment to think about your last six months and write down six things you have accomplished; take pride in them. Be secure in the fact that you are on the right track. God has a purpose for your process.

1. Completed my internship in Los Angeles Emmys

2. Took professional acting/dancing classes

3. Found a mentor that works in my field of interest and has similar qualities, etc.

4. I graduated college a semester early!

5. Learning a new job that I love.

6. Passed all of my classes

I AM ENOUGH

Day 3

I AM Significant

Who I AM

Have you ever struggled with self-esteem? Not the kind of struggle where you don't like your outside appearance, but the struggle of not liking who you are on the inside. At times, we have all felt worthless, full of doubt, and lacking purpose. We let baggage we have collected throughout our lives weigh us down and keep us bound with a "Woe is Me" attitude.

Past hurts from our parents, relatives, relationships, and life experiences, in general, can keep us from fully experiencing life without limits. Many suffer from feelings and fears of rejection, isolation, failure, regrets and the "why-ME's." We collect these feelings along this journey called life and whether we realize it or not, they affect our interactions with others and what we think about ourselves.

Emotional baggage is a heavy load to carry. The excessive weight we walk around with can be detrimental. It often impedes our ability to develop healthy relationships. And hinders our progress in other areas of our personal and professional lives.

My challenge to you today is to decide to get rid of the oppressive, restrictive burden you bear and reclaim your significance.

For some of us, our significance is packaged in our experiences with our parents.
- Were they married? *Nope*
- Did they have a good marriage? *Nope*
- Did you witness domestic abuse? *Yes*
- Did you have an absent father? *emotionally*
- Did you have an emotionally absent parent? *Yes! lol*

For others, our significance is affected by abuse.
- Were you physically abused as a child? *Yes*
- Were you molested or raped? *Yes*
- Were you exposed to pornography as a child? *Yes*
- Did you ever tell anyone? *No*

For others, our significance is affected by our past relationships.

- Were you in an abusive relationship? *No*
- Were you cheated on? *yes*
- Were you manipulated? *No*
- Were you lied to? *yes*

The answers to these questions can logically justify why you feel the way you do. Your feelings of anger, resentment, bitterness, unforgiveness, and other negative emotions may be legitimate. But don't you want something better? Don't you deserve something better?

Truth is you may have learned valuable life-lessons from some of these experiences. You may have also gained wisdom. However, you have to discard the emotional baggage. Lugging with this heavy load will make you lose sight of your significance and may cause many unpleasant side effects such as:

- Anger
- Loss of self-confidence

- Loss of creativity
- Anxiety
- Insecurity
- Sabotaging relationships or attempts at goals
- A constant miserable feeling
- Depression
- Loss of self-respect
- Fear of trying something new
- Lack of trust
- Overwhelming regret

So today, choose a different path. Drop the heavy emotional baggage you have been carrying day after day. Decide to live a life of freedom in Christ Jesus.

Who Does God Say I AM?

The moment you decide to live with true significance, your faith walk will begin. During this walk, you will discover you are not a sum total of your negative experiences. You will realize that God created you with a special, preordained, and specific purpose. The challenges that you faced were not meant to tear you down, but rather, to mold you into a precious vessel for God's glory.

For we are His workmanship, created in Christ Jesus for good works, which God prepared beforehand that we should walk in them (Ephesians 2:10, NKJV).

Practical Application to Become Who I AM

Three tips for getting rid of emotional baggage:

1. **Admit it** – You can fool everyone else, but you can't ever fool yourself. The first step is the same as with any addiction – admittance. Yeah, I did say "addiction." Is emotional baggage an addiction? Maybe not to the scientific world, but you know, as well as I do, that the feelings we get from hanging onto unresolved issues, though not pleasant, provide a comfortable miserableness. It's like that saying, "Better the devil you know than the devil you don't."
2. **See the facts** – Although it is easier to blame the entire world for every problem, eventually, you need to start acknowledging that you make mistakes. And it

is OK to make mistakes. Of course, you can rightfully blame other people for many of the ills that contribute to your emotional baggage. But hanging onto unresolved issues is solely your choice. If you hoard them and refuse to seek help, you can only blame yourself for your unhappiness.

3. **Forgiveness** – After recognizing that you have emotional baggage, understanding exactly where it is coming from and that you are choosing to hang onto it, then the next step is to let it go. It is time to stop blaming and holding resentment against yourself and everyone else. Let go of the anger, pain, blame, bitterness, fear and all other emotions that are stealing your energy. Forgiveness is the greatest healer — forgive yourself and others. You won't ever forget what got you to this point, but forgiveness will disempower its grip on you and set you free to leave it in the past where it belongs.

Note to Who I AM

You are wonderfully made. Don't let past pain rob you of present joy! Get rid of all your emotional baggage and move forward in freedom. Your life has meaning, and you have a purpose. Say out loud: "I AM SIGNIFICANT."

Thrive in who you've been called to *be* without *apology*.
LET'S WORK!

Here's a bit of self-disclosure: I love new handbags! There, I said it. I admit that at times I indulge my purse buying habit a bit too much, but don't tell my husband. Lol! However, today we are going to get a new bag!

We discussed the emotional baggage we have been carrying and the impact it has on our sense of significance. I challenge you to create two lists. On the first list, write down what you've been carrying in your "old bag." List all the pain, rejection, and wounds from your previous experiences. Describe what this bag looks like and how it made you feel. On the second list, write down what you plan to put in your brand-new bag. List the peace, joy, and hopes you have for your future. Describe what this bag looks like and how it makes you feel.

I was carrying this in my OLD BAG:

Childhood traumas

Insecurities

My OLD BAG was:

Childhood memories (that I don't want to remember) - parents abusive relationship - molested - exposed to things at an early age - foot/leg - Weight (too big / too small) - not eating in school - not having a close relationship with my dad. - Dad's drug abuse - Suppressing (smoking weed) - Sister not liking me / jealous of our father living with me - Mother being in & out of the hospital - Dance - Friends snitching up on me - family / cousins can't keep something I tell them to themselves

My OLD BAD made me feel:

Worthless, less than, not in control, like I should be quiet, like I couldn't help, a mistake being here, Worried, anxious, depressed, inadequate, intimidated, Can't trust people (friends or family)

~~last reflections~~

low self-esteem, second-guess everything because I'm more worried about how someone else feels

I will carry this in my NEW BAG: GOD Confidence, healthy relationships, be open to intimate relationships, go-getter spirit, self-worth, Not thinking so hard, care about my feelings put myself first

My NEW BAG will be:

My NEW BAG will help me feel:

Confident in my flaws,

I AM ENOUGH

Day 4

I AM Loved

Who I AM

I was an expert at throwing a pity party when I was younger and didn't get my way. I would sulk all the way to my room, turn off the lights, flop on my bed, and cry for hours. I even had a theme song for my pity party. Want to hear it? Here it goes. Lol!

> I may not be the best at anything
> Nor have the best of everything
> Sometimes I think that I'm the least of all.
> But I know someone who has everything
> And He's my everything
> And I'm happy just to know that I'm His child.

My Aunt Lettie taught that song to the Sunshine Band Choir, and I adopted it as my sad little theme song.

I was so adept at throwing these pity parties because my

concept of love was completely distorted. I thought love was conditional. According to my young mind, if my parents truly loved me, they would give me everything my little heart desired. If they didn't give me what I wanted, they couldn't possibly love me. And surely, if my parents didn't love me, I wasn't worthy of love. Boy, did I have it all wrong.

I wonder how many people still have this warped definition of love. Do we know how to give and receive love? Do you still define love as a barter system based on conditional currency?

Who Does God Say I AM?

"The LORD hath appeared of old unto me, saying, Yea, I have loved thee with an everlasting love: therefore, with lovingkindness have I drawn thee" (Jeremiah 31:3, King James Version).

God is love, and our greatest example of true love. He showed His unconditional love for us by giving His only begotten Son to die for us. That is AMAZING! God has always and will always love us. Such unwavering love baffles the mind.

The key to freely giving love to those around us is fully accepting the love God has for us. Many of us have been hurt by close friends and relatives — those we trust. As a result, we have built walls around our hearts to protect us from ever feeling that pain again. Walls are great for blocking the pain, but they are also great for blocking the love. Yet, the richness and vibrancy of God's love tears down even the tallest walls.

Let's look at the biblical definition of love:

Love is patient and kind; love does not envy or boast; it is not arrogant or rude. It does not insist on its own way; it is not irritable or resentful; it does not rejoice at wrongdoing, but rejoices with the truth. Love bears all things, believes all things, hopes all things, endures all things. Love never ends. (I Corinthians 13:4-8, ESV)

Practical Application to Become Who I AM

How do you define love? Is your concept of love conditional? Do you freely give and receive love? If your ideas about love have been tainted, you need new vision. You need to see love through a new lens — through the eyes of God.

Let your view be free from past hurts, misconceptions, and even the lies that you have told yourself about you. You deserve love.

Note to Who I AM

As we accept the love God so freely gives, I challenge you to love *you* more. Move past all the insecurities you may have collected over the years, accept, and love yourself. Say to yourself: "I am loved, and I am enough."

Thrive in who you've been called to *be* without *apology*.
LET'S WORK!

Let's examine the walls you have built around your heart. Brick by brick, begin to dismantle those walls so you can fully experience the freedom of God's love.

Answer these questions:

Who hurt you?
Father, Sister

How did they hurt you?

Have you forgiven them?

How has this changed the way you love others?

_____
_____
_____

How will you love now?

_____
_____
_____

I AM ENOUGH

Day 5

I AM Chosen

Who I AM

Many of us go through life questioning our purpose. Why am I here? What am I supposed to be doing? Am I using my gifts and talents? What are my gifts and talents? How old will I be before I finally operate in my purpose? Why do all those around me know their purpose, and I don't? Did I miss something? Honestly, we have all asked ourselves these same questions. We have all sought answers about our life purpose in various places and from different people. But the truth of the matter is even if you are not aware of your purpose, God has chosen you.

We may never be innovative masterminds, motivational speakers, or artistic geniuses; however, we have been chosen to change the world in our own ways. You are God's choice. How amazing is that? Out of the billions of people on this earth, God in His infinite wisdom decided to use you at this time, for His purpose. So, as you travel this journey to purpose, hold this reminder close to your heart — I AM CHOSEN.

Who Does God Say I AM?

"Ye have not chosen me, but I have chosen you, and ordained you, that ye should go and bring forth fruit, and that your fruit should remain: that whatsoever ye shall ask of the Father in my name, he may give it you" (John 15:16, King James Version).

I am humbled and amazed to think about God choosing me to be a part of His plan. Despite my flaws, mistakes, and those times when I'm just flat out wrong, He still chose me. It's an honor, privilege, and responsibility to be chosen by God. And guess what? He chose you too! Don't let Him down.

Practical Application to Become Who I AM

You might be thinking, it's great to be chosen, but for what? I still don't know my purpose. Well, this is a great place to press pause. Stop where you are and reflect on a time when you have felt the most fulfilled. What were you doing? Who was there? What did you take away from that moment? Most of us have caught glimpses of our purpose but just didn't recognize them.

Note to Who I AM

At this point, you may reflect on all the times you messed up. You may be thinking, maybe God chose you, but certainly not me. Stop right there. That road of shame and insecurity is closed today! We all have a past. We have all done things we cannot even bear to repeat. However, your past does not define you. Your past can no longer confine you. You have been chosen. Accept it! Walk in it! Go be great!

Thrive in who you've been called to *be* without *apology*.
LET'S WORK!

God has designed a purpose specifically for you that will complement the talents and gifts He has given you.

Take a moment to identify 5 gifts/talents you have.

1. Dance
2. A Love for helping people
3. Creative eye
4.
5.

Write a prayer to God asking Him to direct your path and help you to identify your purpose.

Dear God,

You have gifted me in the areas of

_____

_____

_____

_____

_____

_____

_____

_____

I want to use these gifts to bring You glory and fulfill my purpose on this earth. Show me Your plan for me. Give me clarity and great joy in fulfilling my purpose. Let my will line up with Your will for me. Thank You, God, for choosing me.

In Jesus' name. Amen.

I AM ENOUGH

Day 6

I AM God's Beautiful Creation

Who I AM

"Comparison is the thief of joy" — President Theodore Roosevelt.

Every day, I see women, men, girls, and boys who struggle with low self-esteem. It's a place we all visit at some point in our lives. The falsehoods we claim tear us down little by little and day by day. I am ugly. I am too fat. I am too dark. I am not smart. I am not accomplished. This struggle within ourselves pushes us to search for ways to be more likable, at least, in our minds. We change how we dress, how we wear our hair and even how we talk all in hopes of fitting in with the "in crowd."

Sometimes, it seems to work. However, most of the time it doesn't. You still end up feeling like an outsider because you are trying to fit into this world when you were born to stand out. Why are you going through life in a quest to change exactly who God made you to be. You weren't made to be anyone but you. Acknowledge and accept the person God made you to be. You are His beautiful creation.

Who Does God Say I AM?

"I will praise thee; for I am fearfully and wonderfully made: marvelous are thy works; and that my soul knoweth right well" (Psalm 139:14, KJV).

How many times have I wished to see myself as God sees me? It's so easy to look in the mirror and see flaws, blemishes, shortcomings, and failures. It's much harder to see yourself through the eyes of our loving Father. But, you can do it! From this day forward, I challenge you to change your view of you.

Practical Application to Become Who I AM

You are an ANOMALY. An anomaly is a deviation from the normal or usual order, irregular, unexpected, unusual. It is perfectly OK that you are not like anyone else around you. You weren't ever supposed to be a carbon copy. You are a uniquely designed individual. Appreciate being an anomaly. In fact, love being an anomaly.

Note to Who I AM

In school, do you remember taking tests and hearing your teacher say, "Keep your eyes on your own paper"? Why did she have to say that? Because some people were looking to others for the answers. My challenge to you today is to stop looking to others for validation. Keep your eyes on your purpose. You don't need others' opinions when you already have the ANSWERS!

Thrive in who you've been called to be without apology.
LET'S WORK!

4 A's to seeing yourself as God sees you:

ACKNOWLEDGE: Take a moment to acknowledge how you have been viewing yourself. At first glance in the mirror, is your view negative or positive? Write down what you see.

_____
_____
_____
_____
_____
_____
_____
_____

AGREE: Agree that your view is warped by insecurities, doubts, and lies that you have allowed yourself to believe.

ASK: Ask God to change your view. Ask Him to help you see the beauty and wonder of His creation — YOU!

ACCEPT: Accept that it is time to change the channel! You have seen this re-run for the last time. Now is the time for you to be all that you can be. You deserve it. You are God's beautiful creation.

I AM ENOUGH

Day 7

I AM Strong

Who I AM

I have faced trials, challenges, and troubles just like everyone else. I've been disappointed, frustrated, and disheartened. I have wanted to quit, run away, and sometimes, stay in bed all week. Yet, I am strong. I found the strength to pull it together, to get up and try again. Where did my strength come from?

I wish I could tell you I'm just so amazing I never let anything keep me down. But that's not true. I've simply learned the secret, and I'm going to share it with you, just because I love you so much: I ask for help. Whenever I am at my lowest points, I realize that I have direct access to an all-powerful God who is not only willing but able to come to my rescue.

God knows exactly how to heal every hurt and make your heart whole again. He knows precisely how to pick up the pieces and make a masterpiece out of your mess. He knows when to send your tribe when you feel alone in tribulation. I am so grateful that in the worst times, in Him, I am strong.

Who Does God Say I AM?

"And he said unto me, my grace is sufficient for thee: for my strength is made perfect in weakness. Most gladly therefore will I rather glory in my infirmities, that the power of Christ may rest upon me" (II Corinthians 12:9, KJV).

Amazing grace seems to be such an understatement. There are really no words to accurately describe God's sovereignty and sufficiency. I'm so glad that no matter how bad my situation seems, He's always there to rescue me.

Practical Application to Become Who I AM

Choose to accept the strength God offers. Take it for your own. Look ahead with hope. As you do, soak in the peace it gives you. Strength is not just about overcoming your circumstances. It's about learning a lesson through your weaknesses.

Note to Who I AM

Confession time: I am a huge Wonder Woman fan. I love everything about Wonder Woman including her amazing costume, lasso of truth, her red boots, and her gold bracelets but most of all, her strength.

Wonder Woman always defeats her foes and comes out victorious looking fabulous. However, even Wonder Woman has a weakness. If a man ties her bracelets together, she will lose her superhuman strength. So even Wonder Woman needs help sometimes.

Stop expecting to be strong all the time. It's alright to break down occasionally. In fact, it is natural. We need to be real with ourselves, with each other, and with God. If we share our struggles with each other we give people the permission to help us. We open doors to healing and relief.

Thrive in who you've been called to be without apology.
LET'S WORK!

Underneath the façade, many women are hurting and grieving. On the surface, it seems as if everything is fine. However, they live each day feeling insecure, inadequate, and unloved or unworthy of love. They hide these feelings and try to be strong. If you are one of these women please understand that you are not alone.

To endure the pain of our circumstances, we tend to do things we *think* will help us feel better. Needless to say, many times, these things only bring temporary relief. What do you do when you feel weak? Are you an emotional eater or an impulsive shopper? Do you isolate yourself or do you keep busy to avoid your feelings?

Take a moment and be honest with yourself. Answer the following questions:

What do you do when you feel weak?

Sleep, overthink, second-guess, don't eat, quiet

What will help you feel stronger?

- Being good at things I do (job, dance, work, etc.)
- Not worrying about the other person so much

Have you asked God to help you in your times of weakness? Why or why not?

Yes because I had felt like I hit rock bottom and had no one to turn to.
No, because I felt like He couldn't hear me or He was tired of me.

I AM ENOUGH

Day 8

I AM Capable

Who I AM

Some of us constantly battle internally with skill and will. We have the training, education, and experience but doubt if we can really make it happen. We brag about our Alma mater and proudly wear our school colors. (Shout out to Whitney M. Young High school and The University of Illinois). However, when the rubber meets the road, we get scared and stuck. The skill is there, but the will is weak. It's easy to cycle through doubt, fear, procrastination, and ultimately, self-sabotage. It takes real courage to push past all those feelings and fully embrace this statement: I AM CAPABLE!

I am assuming that most of you are like me. You wear numerous hats on any given day. Mother, wife, sister, daughter, friend, counselor, church member, employee, employer, entrepreneur, business owner, driver, cook, maid, and the beat goes on. I always have a to-do list that is a mile long. Things to do for work, things to do for home, groceries to buy, kids programs to attend, committees to serve on, emails and texts to send, phone calls and appointments to make. Help! Yes, I know how to do all these things; however, sometimes — OK, a lot of the time, I become very overwhelmed with life and wonder if I can really make it happen.

Who Does God Say I AM?

I can do all things through Christ which strengtheneth me (Philippians 4:13, KJV).

God's Word literally says that I AM CAPABLE. God will strengthen and enable you to do any and everything. We must trust that He has fully equipped us to accomplish our goals. Nothing is impossible with His help.

Practical Application to Become Who I AM

Five steps to make you feel capable:
1. Stop over-committing yourself. Stop saying yes to the things you have no interest or desire in doing.

2. Don't look at the big picture. Instead, pick five things on your to-do list each day and get them done. If you don't get them done, don't beat yourself up; just put them on the list for the next day and — GET THEM DONE.

3. Reward yourself when you get your list completed. Read that magazine or book that you have been waiting to read. Take a long hot bath. Eat a cookie… just one.

4. Make your schedule more realistic. There really are only 24 hours in a day. Allow time for meals, travel, and — oh, yeah — breathing.

5. Finally, get started. If you don't start, you will never finish.

Note to Who I AM

My first-grade teacher, Mrs. Jackson was such an amazing motivator. Every morning she would have our entire class stand and say, "I can do it. I can do it if I put my mind to it." Years later, when I doubt myself and feel overwhelmed or incapable, I stand up and with all my first-grade hand motions. I remind myself that I can do it!

You see, Mrs. Jackson knew that at just six years old, we would face challenges and doubt our capabilities. She may never know how that morning mantra shifted my life trajectory, but I'm so grateful for her.

Thrive in who you've been called to *be* without *apology*.
LET'S WORK!

Everyone needs some encouragement along the way, even if you must encourage yourself. You need to be reminded that you have the skills; you can do it, and you are CAPABLE. Do you have a favorite scripture or song that gives you that extra pep in your step? If you don't, now is the perfect moment to discover it. Let's go!

1. Write down 3 scriptures that encourage you.

2. Write down 3 songs that encourage you.

When you feel unsure or incapable refer to these lists and use this encouragement to propel you forward. Remember to say to yourself, I AM CAPABLE.

I AM ENOUGH

Day 9

I AM Bold

Who I AM

I am BOLD. I chuckle a little bit even as I write because that was never a word I would use to describe myself. In fact, growing up, I was always quite the opposite. You see, in my mind, bold means powerful, fearless, and brave. When I think of a bold person, I think of someone who is outspoken, charismatic, and in your face. That has never been me. My family will tell you that I have always been easily frightened, and that's putting it mildly. They would probably call me a scary cat. Loud and unexpected noises, clowns, spiders, the dark, I could go on, but I won't. Oh, the stories my siblings could tell. However, I've gotten older and hopefully, a little wiser. I have realized that life can be scary at times, and that's OK.

Fear is a healthy emotion that can keep us safe. However, irrational fear can keep us paralyzed in doubt, insecurity, and falsehoods. Fear is often a distraction that keeps you consumed with the minor details, instead of focusing on the big picture. As a result, I have redefined what being bold means to me. For me, bold means **B**elieving that I can **O**vercome **L**ife's **D**istractions with the help of the Lord. I am so glad I finally realized that if I walk with God, I don't have to operate in fear. I AM BOLD.

Who Does God Say I AM?

"According to the eternal purpose which he purposed in Christ Jesus our Lord: In whom we have boldness and access with confidence by the faith of him. Wherefore I desire that ye faint not at my tribulations for you, which is your glory" (Ephesians 3:11-13, KJV).

I am so glad that I don't have to rely on my strength to have boldness. I can be confident in my glorious Savior, who always has my back. No matter what I face or how scary it may look, God is right there with me. Even though my knees may be knocking loudly together, I know that with His help — I AM BOLD.

Practical Application to Become Who I AM

Walking in fear is like walking into a dark room with a flashlight in your hand but never turning it on. You have the source of light in your hand but you won't use it.

Jesus is the Light of the world. Let Him illuminate your life. Let His love and grace shine a light on your insecurities, doubts, and areas of unbelief. Let Him show you how to be BOLD. With the help of God, we can Believe and Overcome Life's Distractions.

Note to Who I AM

It's never too late to overcome a fear that has held you hostage. Just because you may have had held on to it thus far, doesn't mean you must keep holding it. It's time to stop merely existing in fear and start living BOLDLY in freedom. Today is your day!

Thrive in who you've been called to *be* without *apology*.
LET'S WORK!

I have some GREAT NEWS for you! You can overcome your fears and be BOLD. Some of us have been trapped by fear for very long, but it's time to be free. Today begins your journey of facing the fears, fixing what you face and being FREE.

Start here:

Put a name on the fears that have kept you distracted from reaching your goals. Then, if you can, explain why you have held on to this fear so long. Now, this may require some time and self-reflection but stick with it. It's worth the work. Finally, being BOLD requires that you take just one step toward freedom. Identify your first step in moving past these fears.

FEAR #1:

_____
_____
_____

Why have I been afraid?

_____
_____
_____

My First step toward Freedom from this Fear is:

_____
_____
_____

FEAR #2:

_____
_____
_____

Why have I been afraid?

_____

_____

_____

My First step toward Freedom from this Fear is:

_____

_____

_____

I AM ENOUGH

Day 10

I AM Living with Purpose

Who I AM

About three years ago, something awakened in me, and I decided I was going to do life differently. Perhaps, it was the idea of turning 40 or maybe, I was just tired of going through the motions of life. I wanted to change. I was in a place where I was finally open to living just as God had ordained. So often, we live based on the expectations of others. We also live based on our dreams, goals or self-imposed expectations. But I wanted a change. I desired to live on purpose and with purpose — God's purpose.

My wakeup call was the timeline I created some time during my early 20's. I was supposed to be married by 25, have 2 kids by 30, and be well-established in my career by 35. I had so many well-intentioned and lofty goals.

I read somewhere that God laughs when we make plans. I can imagine Him laughing at me right now. I had this straight and narrow path lined up for my life, but I had no idea the detours, re-routing and dead ends that I would encounter. I thought I had it all figured out and boy, was I wrong. I soon found out that I was not really living until I yielded all these plans to God. Ultimately, I realized that God is, was, and forever will be in control of my life. Now I can say that I am living on purpose.

Who Does God Say I AM?

"For we are His workmanship [His own masterwork, a work of art], created in Christ Jesus [reborn from above—spiritually transformed, renewed, ready to be used] for good works, which God prepared [for us] beforehand [taking paths which He set], so that we would walk in them [living the good life which He prearranged and made ready for us]" (Ephesians 2:10, AMP).

It's so humbling and wonderful to know that God made a plan. And even if I don't know all the details, and I may question it every step of the way, He still includes me in His plan.

Practical Application to Become Who I AM

In my crazy imagination, I picture myself on a road trip with God. Of course, He's driving, and I'm the annoying child in the backseat whining. Every ten miles or so, I'm questioning, "Are we there yet?" God never loses patience with me and yells, "Shut up, and don't ask me again!" like I would with my sons. Instead, He calmly responds, "It will be worth the wait, my child."

When we let God lead, our journeys to purpose are much smoother.

Note to Who I AM

You were particularly designed for a spectacular purpose. You may not always have the step by step directions, and at times, that's very frustrating. However, you can take comfort in the fact that you know the map maker! Each turn and twist on your journey is leading you right where He wants you to be. There is a plan and a purpose.

Thrive in who you've been called to *be* without *apology*.

LET'S WORK!

A big part of living with purpose is allowing your will to line up with God's will. That's no easy task, but it's worth the work. So, let's do it.

➢ **W - Wait in stillness**

Be still. This is something you will constantly have to remind yourself to do. You don't *have* to move right now. You don't *have* to decide right now. Challenge yourself in this area.

I can wait for God to show me:

_____

_____

_____

_____

_____

_____

_____

➢ I - Increase your quiet time

As you are waiting, increase your quiet time in prayer and studying the Word. Set aside a time you will dedicate to God.

My new time for prayer and devotion is:

_____

_____

➢ L - Listen for and learn His voice

When you are quiet, you can hear God's directions. Allow Him to speak to you and guide you during your time with Him.

I'm listening God. What is my purpose?

_____

_____

_____

_____

➤ L - Lean not to your own understanding

Ask God to make His will clear to you. When He does, you still may not understand everything. Remember His ways are above our ways and His thoughts are above our thoughts (Isaiah 55:8). So don't go by what makes sense to you. He has you just where He wants you.

I trust You God, and I want to live with purpose. Help me to understand this:

_____
_____
_____
_____
_____

I AM ENOUGH

Day 11

I AM forgiven

Who I AM

"Forgiveness is not an occasional act, it is a constant attitude"
— Dr. Martin Luther King Jr.

WOW! JUST…WOW! Now that is deep and honestly, a bit out of my grasp. In my mind, when I forgive someone for what I consider a major offense, it's a big deal. There is no greater reminder of how much I really need God, than when someone intentionally wrongs me. Look, I can be completely honest with you; my first reaction is to hold a grudge. I have a wicked side-eye, and I'm not afraid to use it over and over again.

However, I've concluded that God really loves me because He keeps giving me opportunities to get it together. I finally understand that forgiving others is not giving them a free pass or condoning their behaviors. Forgiveness is freeing yourself from the hurt, bitterness, and anger the offense has caused you. Forgiveness is your passport to healing. It allows you to move on, even if it still hurts.

Perhaps, the hardest part of forgiveness is forgiving you. We have made some choices that we won't let ourselves get over. We constantly hold them over our heads and bring them up every chance we get. We beat the dead horse, resurrect it, and beat it again! This cycle must end. To be forgiven, we must forgive. Yes, this means that we must forgive ourselves.

Today, let's shake off the shackles of unforgiveness and let's say together, "I AM FORGIVEN!"

Who Does God Say I AM?
"If you, GOD, kept records on wrongdoings, who would stand a chance? As it turns out, forgiveness is your habit, and that's why you're worshiped" (Psalm 130:3-4, MSG).

"There is therefore now no condemnation to them which are in Christ Jesus, who walk not after the flesh, but after the Spirit" (Romans 8:1, KJV).

The grace of God is astounding. He continues to forgive and forget. I'm so glad that His ways are not our ways and His thoughts are not our thoughts. Otherwise, we would be in TROUBLE.

Practical Application to Become Who I AM
To make forgiveness a constant attitude, we must continually work on it. Don't beat yourself up or give up just because you don't get it right every time. Instead, decide to keep trying to be better. Start today; don't wait. You might have to forgive someone else tomorrow. LOL!

Note to Who I AM
Unforgiveness has a way of clouding your vision. It's like looking out of a window that is smeared with mud. The sun doesn't seem to shine as bright, and the flowers don't seem as pretty. However, when you forgive, your vision clears and

your perspective changes. You deserve an opportunity to see things differently.

I AM ENOUGH

Thrive in who you've been called to *be* without *apology*.

LET'S WORK!

As we grow in grace and learn to forgive consistently, we must begin the work on ourselves. Release the guilt of past mistakes, failures, and outcomes of circumstances beyond your control. Write a forgiveness letter to yourself that grants you freedom from all thoughts and actions you have yet to let go. Put the note in an envelope, but don't seal it. You may need to read it again in order to remain in a forgiving state. Write your preliminary thoughts here:

Dear Me,

I forgive you for:

_____

_____

_____

_____

_____

_____

_____

Day 12

I AM at Peace

Who I AM

Peace of mind is priceless. It can't be traded, borrowed or purchased. Peace is not dependent on your present circumstances. Rather, it relies on your mindset. Peace is a decision you make based on your confidence and faith in God.

The reality is pressure is a part of life. It is inevitable. However, you must decide how to deal with it. One of my favorite artists, Jonathan McReynolds penned a song that expresses the sentiments of so many people I talk to every day.

> I can't even turn on my phone
> Without being reminded of the lie
> That I am alone and broken, unsuccessful.
> I can't always talk to my friends
> Cause they've got expectations

That I may or may not be living up to.

I really need to rid myself, of the pressure, pressure, pressure

To be someone else that the world has made

Jesus take from me all the pressure, pressure, pressure

To be someone that you did not create.

You need to adjust your expectations of yourself. Stop letting society influence and dictate how your "happy" should look. Take a step back and re-evaluate your priorities. How do you really want your life to look? What fulfills you? After you've answered these questions, gradually discard, cancel, and get rid of all the other unnecessary things that have been blocking your path to peace. You must decide to declare, "I AM AT PEACE."

Who Does God Say I AM?

"And the peace of God, which passeth all understanding, shall keep your hearts and minds through Christ Jesus" (Philippians 4:7, KJV).

"Not that I speak in respect of want: for I have learned, in whatsoever state I am, therewith to be content" (Philippians 4:11, KJV).

The peace of God is a precious commodity. His peace will help you make it through situations that seem insurmountable. His peace will bring you comfort in your darkest hours. His peace will stabilize you in the most tumultuous times. It's beyond our comprehension, and yet, something we strive for daily.

Practical Application to Become Who I AM

Here are a few tips to decrease the pressures of life:

1. Set realistic expectations for yourself. Stop looking at others. Rather, realize and accept how awesome you really are. You don't have to be the soccer mom, the organic chef, and the craft guru. Pick a hobby, sport or some other thing you love and do it well. Some days, do nothing. Laze around, order the pizza, and binge as you watch your favorite show.

2. Don't answer the phone every time someone calls. You have voicemail for a reason. Use it! You know which phone calls you have to answer. Answer the other calls when you have more time.

3. Schedule off days for yourself. You push yourself to the limit most days. Give yourself a day off from everything except the basic necessities and **don't feel guilty about it**.

4. If you need help, ask for it. Our friends and families are not mind readers. They may be more than willing to help if they knew there was a need.

5. Take off the cape. No one is expecting Wonder Woman to show up every day, except — maybe you.

Note to Who I AM

We all have pressure points. These are the sensitive areas in our lives that can cause the most stress. It may be our careers, children, relationships or financial status. Somewhere along this journey of life, we have convinced ourselves that we always need more. Don't get me wrong; ambition and drive are good. However, when your mission is to get more or be more just to show everyone how great you are, then Houston, we have a problem. A significant step in preserving, protecting, and maintaining your peace is learning how to be content.

I AM ENOUGH

Thrive in who you've been called to be without apology.

LET'S WORK!

What are your "pressure points"?

_____

_____

_____

_____

_____

What can you do to preserve, protect and/or maintain your peace?

_____

_____

_____

_____

_____

Day 13

I AM Whole

Who I AM

As we go through life, we experience the good and the bad, the highs and lows. Then there are the trials that make us feel as if we are literally being ripped to shreds. Perhaps, it was the loss of a parent. Maybe it was being sexually assaulted. Or maybe you were in an abusive relationship. Maybe your marriage is in trouble. Maybe you lost your job and are in danger of losing it all. How do you put yourself back together when you feel as if you have nothing left? How do you recover from the anxiety or depression that threatens to consume you?

As a child of God, a believer, a saint, how do you put the pieces back together? Where do you turn for help? Many of God's children are fighting battles on their own because they are too ashamed or afraid to ask for help. You know how to fast and pray, but do you know when you need to seek counseling? There is such a stigma surrounding therapy in the Christian faith. Some believers feel that going to counseling negates the power of God. But it does not. You can pray, believe, have faith and go to counseling to work through your issues. There are licensed, trained, and Bible-believing therapists who can help you put the pieces back together. With their help and the help of God who is the wonderful counselor, you can say, "I AM WHOLE."

Who Does God Say I AM?

"When Jesus saw him lie, and knew that he had been now a long time in that case, he saith unto him, Wilt thou be made whole?" (John 5:6, KJV).

You know the story of the man by the pool of Bethesda. He struggled with his sickness for 38 years. Jesus asked him, "Wilt thou be made whole." He told Jesus that he had no one to put him in the pool, and people kept getting in front of him in the line. Jesus told him, "Rise, take up thy bed and walk."

Practical Application to Become Who I AM

It is important to be whole in your mind, body, and soul. If you are struggling right now, know that you are not alone. You don't have to suffer in silence. There is support for you. There is help for you. There is hope for you. You can be WHOLE.

Note to Who I AM

Are you hiding your depression, anxiety, low self-esteem, a history of abuse or your eating disorder? What are you hiding? And even more importantly, why are you hiding? You can't worry about what others may say or think. Nothing is more important than being made WHOLE.

Thrive in who you've been called to *be* without *apology*.

LET'S WORK!

A strong person knows when to ask for help. If you are struggling or you feel broken, don't be afraid to reach out. Here are a few things you can do:

- Pray and ask God to lead and direct you to the right person to help with your issues.
- Search for a therapist in your area whom you would feel comfortable talking to.
- Use your resources. Ask for a referral from your primary care physician.
- Most importantly, believe that you will be made WHOLE.

I AM ENOUGH

Day 14

I AM me & I AM enough

Who I AM

The time comes in everyone's life when you stop living for other people. You stop putting on a mask for work, another one for church, friends, family or even for social media. What a freeing moment it is when you decide to be your authentic self! When this shift occurs, your perspective changes. You begin to realize what you like or dislike. You become more grounded in your social and political agendas. You even become more rooted in your faith.

Simply put, you stop living your life based on the opinions of others. People had opinions before you were born and will continue to have them long after you leave this world. So instead of trying to portray yourself, decide to just BE yourself. If you have not come to the place of self-acceptance, this is a perfect time to start. Take some time today to re-establish your relationship with you. Take off the masks and be real with yourself. Are you a people pleaser?

Do you have some unresolved issues, hurts, or situations that need immediate attention? Whatever it is, take the mask off and deal with it. Journal it, pray about it, and go to therapy. Do whatever you need to do to truly believe and be able to say, "I AM ME AND I AM ENOUGH!"

Who Does God Say I AM?

> O Lord, thou hast searched me, and known me. Thou knowest my downsitting and mine uprising, thou understandest my thought afar off. Thou compassest my path and my lying down, and art acquainted with all my ways. For there is not a word in my tongue, but, lo, O LORD, thou knowest it altogether. Thou hast beset me behind and before, and laid thine hand upon me. Such knowledge is too wonderful for me; it is high, I cannot attain unto it (Psalm 139, KJV).

I don't know about you, but it amazes me that God knows everything about me and still loves me with an amazing all-encompassing love. God knows all the deep dark stuff that we push to the back of the closets of our minds and memories. He knows every shameful thought, memory, and mistake. Yet, He loves us just as we are. There is no greater love than His love for us. It humbles me to the point of tears to know that no matter what I think about myself, God thinks that I AM ENOUGH.

Practical Application to Become Who I AM

At times in life, you will feel unworthy, incapable, and inadequate. These are all normal emotions that everyone has experienced at some point in life. The best thing that you can do for yourself is to acknowledge the feeling and then move from that place. If allowed to fester, these emotions begin to spread like a virus and will affect your life perspective. If you need help to get past your stinking-thinking, talk to a friend, loved one or a therapist. We can all benefit from being reminded that our mistakes don't define who we are or who we are becoming.

Note to Who I AM

A wise man once told me, "To love someone is to give them room to grow." I challenge you to love yourself enough to give you room to grow. As you grow, you will mess up and sometimes fail, but don't beat yourself up. Love yourself through the valleys, pitfalls, and dark places. You are growing, and you are ENOUGH.

I AM ENOUGH

Thrive in who you've been called to be without apology.

LET'S WORK!

This is our last activity, and I'm asking you to dig deep for this one. Find a quiet place where you can be alone. Think about those moments and situations that you thought were too terrible to come back from. Think about those times when you were embarrassed and ashamed of yourself. Think about those things you have never told anyone and probably never will. Whew, it is heavy, right?

Now think of the ways that God has shown His love for you despite it all. List them here:

_____

_____

_____

_____

_____

_____

_____

List the ways He shows you that He loves your flaws and all.

___

___

___

___

___

___

___

List the ways He continues to show you that you are His child and **YOU ARE ENOUGH!**

___

___

___

___

___

___

___

CONCLUSION

Thanks so much for joining me on this 14-day journey of self-discovery. It's my hope that this is just the beginning and you will continue the quest of coming to a full awareness of how uniquely wonderful and powerful you truly are. You have everything that you need inside of you to be great right now. Simply accept and activate it. So many of us remain bound by our fears, insecurities, and doubts. This must change.

Let me share with you the moment things began to shift for me and I literally got out of my own way. Last summer, I was reading Shonda Rhimes book, *Year of Yes*. If you haven't read it, do yourself a favor and get it. It is hilarious.

While reading it, I began to wonder what would happen if I said YES to everything God has for me. It seemed so simple in theory, but in practice, it was a big ol' scary thought. It meant that I had to get rid of all the excuses and utter foolishness I allowed to sidetrack me. It meant that I had to learn how to trust and depend on God. It also meant that I had to silence the doubters and shift my circle of influencers. My grandfather always said that it's difficult to soar with eagles if you are hanging with turkeys. I learned that you can't share everything with everyone. I have never been concerned with haters, but I do know that there are dream killers out there. These are the people who are quick to discourage, criticize and list all the reasons why your dream won't work. Beware of these people.

Identify your cheerleaders and put them in the front row. My goal is to empower individuals who will, in turn, strengthen their families, communities, places of worship, schools, and the world. We all need to be reminded that we are enough!

As you continue your journey, please, stay in contact with me and update me on your progress. *I Am Enough* is not just a book; it's a MOVEMENT!

Until next time, may His grace sustain you, His mercy keep you and His love surround you!

ABOUT THE AUTHOR

Chantelle Bittings is a lifetime member of the Rehoboth Ministries Church of God in Christ, in Park Forest, IL. She serves in various positions in the church including the Minister of Music, Youth Leader, personal secretary to the pastor and wherever she can be of service to the ministry.

She is the devoted wife to Elder Thomas Bittings, and the mother of two sons, Thomas and Gaston Bittings. She is a Licensed Clinical Professional Counselor and finds great joy in helping others. Chantelle Bittings has been dedicated to providing quality mental health services since 2001.

She is a graduate of the University of Illinois in Champaign-Urbana with a Bachelor's degree in psychology. She obtained her master's degree in Counseling Psychology from the Illinois School of Professional Psychology in 2001 and is a Licensed Clinical Professional Counselor in the State of Illinois. She is also a National Certified Counselor. In her practice, she provides individual and family therapy and empowers others to make effective changes in their lives.

Visit her website: *www.cbittingstherapy.com*